MOVING ART

Hilary Devonshire

Consultant: Henry Pluckrose

Photography: Chris Fairclough

FRANKLIN WATTS
New York/London/Sydney/Toronto

Copyright © 1990 Franklin Watts

Franklin Watts Inc
387 Park Avenue South
New York
NY 10016

Library of Congress Cataloging-in-Publication Data

Devonshire, Hilary.
    Moving art / Hilary Devonshire.
        p.   cm. — (Fresh start)
    Summary: Shows how to construct mobiles, pop-ups, dolls, animals,
and other moving objects, using different types of paper, foils, and
fabrics.
    ISBN 0-531-14076-8
    1. Paper work—Juvenile literature.   2. Kinetic art—Juvenile
literature.   [1. Handicraft.   2. Kinetic art.]   I. Title.
II. Series: Fresh start (London, England)
TT870.D43   1990
745.54—dc20   90-31637
                                                         CIP AC

Design: K & Co

Editor: Jenny Wood

Typeset by Lineage Ltd,
Watford, England

Printed in Belgium

Contents

Equipment and materials

This book describes activities which use the following:

Adhesives – clear cold water paste (wallpaper paste), white glue (such as Elmer's)
Beads
Bottle (with its cork)
Brushes (for glue and paint)
Cardboard (thin white and colored cardboard, and thick cardboard)
Cardboard boxes
Cardboard tubes
Compass (for drawing circles)
Craft knife
Crayons
Dowel rod
Fabric (soft, thin material such as nylon, polyester, silk, and assorted scraps)
Felt-tip pens (a selection of colors)
Garden stakes
Hole punch
Junk materials (such as assorted waste packaging)
Masking tape
Matchboxes
Modeling clay
Needle
Newspaper (old)

Paint (acrylic, poster or powder)
Paper (white and colored)
Paper fasteners
Paper plates
Pastels (oil)
Pencil
Ping-pong ball
Pin (long)
Plastic bowl (an old one, for mixing papier mâché)
Plates (one large, one small, for drawing round)
Ribbons
Rubber bands
Ruler (wooden or plastic, and metal for use with the craft knife)
Scissors
Sequins
Sticky tape
String (thin)
Thread (such as cotton thread or embroidery thread)
Tray (round)
Wrapping paper (patterned)
Yarn
Yogurt cartons

Getting ready

I decided to call this book *Moving Art* because in each model or design there is some part which moves, or gives the impression of movement. Some of the ideas described are optical illusions, a trick of the eye. Others are three-dimensional and, therefore, more lifelike.

Action or movement in a picture or model can make it much more exciting. You can also use the action or movement to create a surprise within the picture or model – see, for example, the pop-up figure on pages 20-23.

The card or toy that you make could be a present for a friend or relative. You could surprise them too!

When you have experimented with the ideas in this book, and discovered how the movement occurs, try to use the techniques to develop new models and designs of your own. Turning an idea into something new is being truly creative. Have fun!

1 Important pieces of equipment.

A rocking design

You will need some thin white cardboard, a pen or pencil, a round tray, crayons, white glue and a glue brush.

1 Place your tray on the white cardboard and draw around part of the rim to make the curved base for your picture.

2 Draw your picture and color it in.

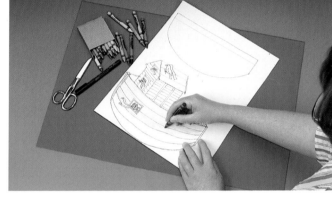

3 Cut out another piece of cardboard with a matching curved base. This will support your picture so that it will stand up. Draw a line 1cm (⅜″) from the top edge.

4 Fold along this line and brush glue along the edge.

5 Attach the cardboard support to the back of your picture so that the two base edges are parallel.

6 *"Noah's Ark."* Push the ark and watch it rock.

Here are some ideas for other rocking designs:
a) a balancing juggler,
b) a swimming duck,
c) a rocking cradle.

A rotating scene

In this scene you will be able to change the weather from sun to snow! You will need three pieces of thin white cardboard, a pencil, a ruler, a compass, scissors, paints, paintbrushes, a paper fastener, Elmer's glue and a glue brush.

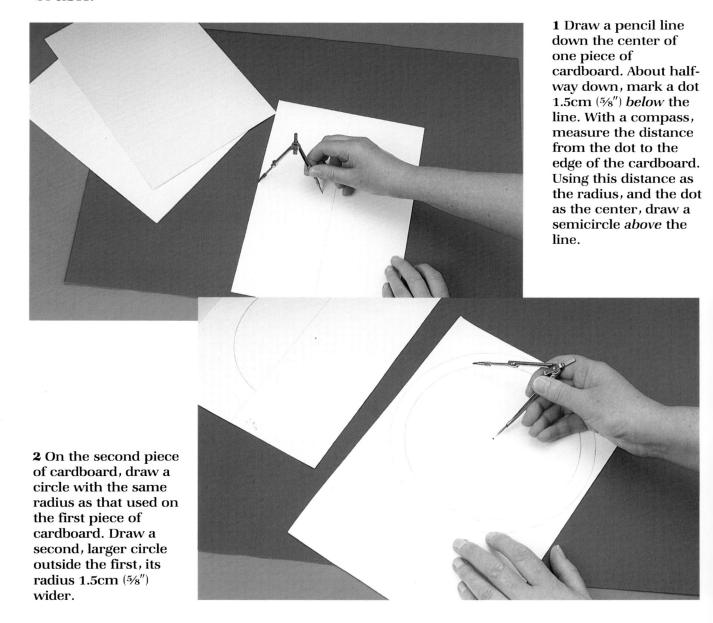

1 Draw a pencil line down the center of one piece of cardboard. About halfway down, mark a dot 1.5cm (⅝") *below* the line. With a compass, measure the distance from the dot to the edge of the cardboard. Using this distance as the radius, and the dot as the center, draw a semicircle *above* the line.

2 On the second piece of cardboard, draw a circle with the same radius as that used on the first piece of cardboard. Draw a second, larger circle outside the first, its radius 1.5cm (⅝") wider.

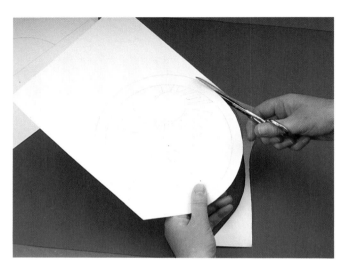

3 Draw a sun in one half of the inner circle, and snowflakes in the other half. Cut out your circle, around the outer edge.

4 Draw a scene around the semicircle on the first piece of cardboard...

5 ...then cut away the semicircular space.

6 Paint your scene. Paint the sky and sun in the circle, too, adding a decorative border if you like.

7 Push the paper fastener through the dot below the line...

8 ...then through the center of the circle and, finally, through a spare piece of cardboard cut to a square. Open out the fastener.

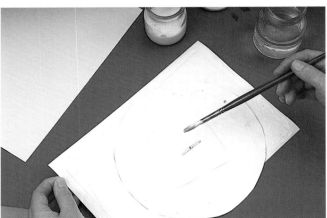

9 Glue around the paper fastener on the square piece of cardboard, and also around the edges of the back of your picture.

10 Mount your picture onto the third piece of cardboard. Press firmly and leave to dry.

11 The cardboard circle will rotate inside the scene. Here the sun is shining...

12 ...and here the snow has started to fall!

When the frog's mouth opens and shuts, it appears to be talking. You can design fun greeting cards using this idea.

You will need paper, crayons, scissors, glue, and some heavy paper or cardboard for mounting.

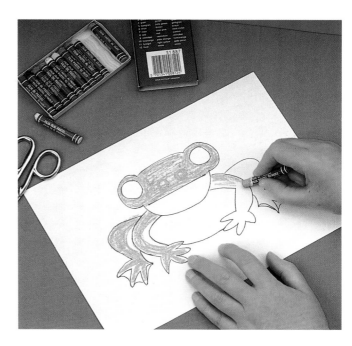

1 Draw and color your frog (or any creature of your choice). Make sure your drawing is as symmetrical as possible, on either side of the center of the paper.

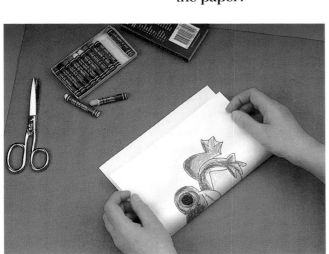

2 Keeping the picture of the frog on the outside, fold the paper in half and...

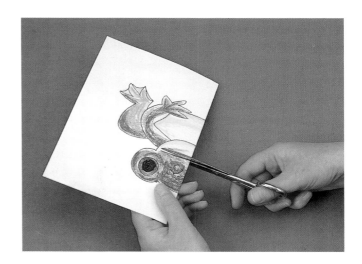

3 ...cut along the line of the frog's mouth.

4 Fold back a triangle of paper at the top and bottom of the mouth.

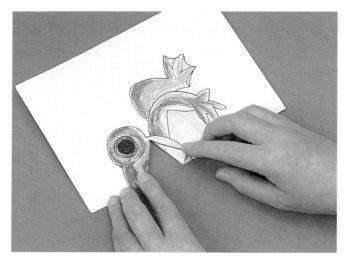

5 Open out your picture then fold it in half again, this time with the frog on the inside. Push the folded triangles of the mouth forward.

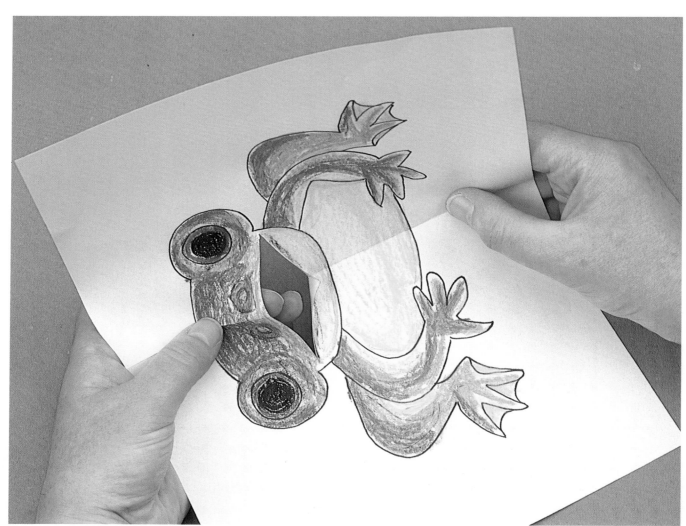

6 Close the paper and press firmly along the folds of the mouth (which are now folded back inside).

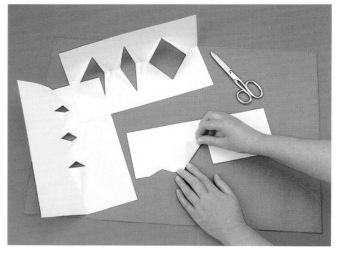

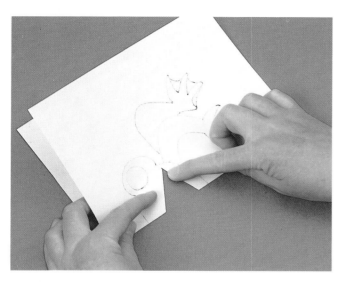

7 You can experiment with different lengths of cuts and larger triangular folds. Some mouths will open wide, others will be like small beaks.

8 Stick your frog onto a piece of thick cardboard (or heavy paper) that has been folded along the center.

9 As you open and close the card, the frog's mouth will open and shut. The owl in the background has a moving, pointed beak made in the same way.

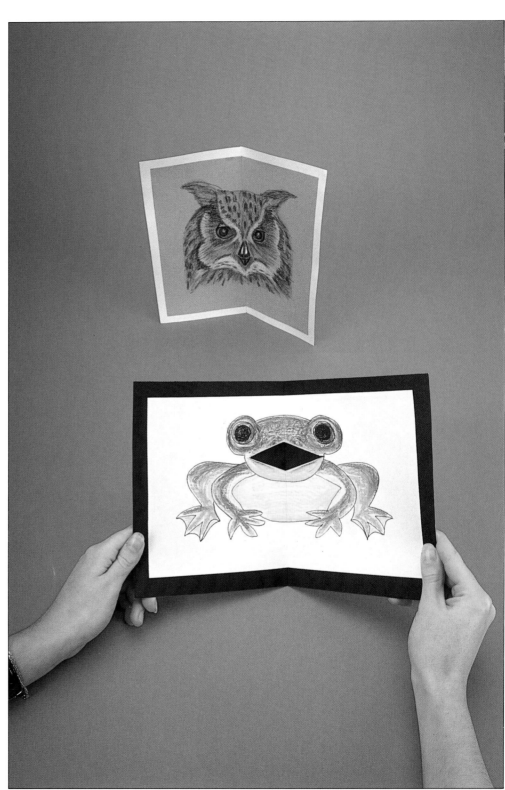

Make a character with moving arms, or a bird with flapping wings! You will need thin white card, a pencil, felt-tip pens, scissors, two paper fasteners, a needle, embroidery silk and a bead.

1 Draw the body of your character on a piece of cardboard. Draw the two arms separately. Color your figure with felt-tip pens.

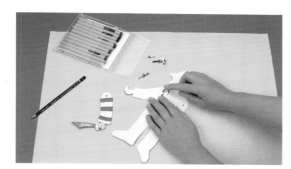

2 Cut out your figure and loosely attach the arms at the shoulders with the two paper fasteners.

3 Using the needle, thread a length of embroidery silk through the top of the arms above the paper fasteners.

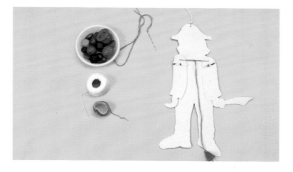

4 With the arms hanging straight down, tie the thread so that it is tight across the back of the figure. Leave a long piece of thread to use as a pull. Tie a bead on the end of the thread.

5 *The Pirate* The finished figure.

6 When you pull the thread, the pirate will raise his arms. The second figure shown here was created from a sketch drawn in a museum. Can you make a figure which moves both arms *and* legs?

7 Here is another idea.
A decorated chick...

8 ...bursts from its
egg!

Pop-up art – a pop-up figure

Pop-up designs are a popular way of making cards which contain a surprise when they are opened. For this idea you will need thin, white cardboard, felt-tip pens, scissors, a small quantity of Elmer's glue and a glue brush.

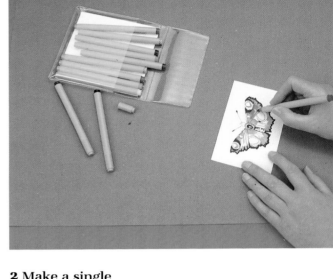

1 Draw a figure (a person or creature) on a postcard-size piece of the cardboard.

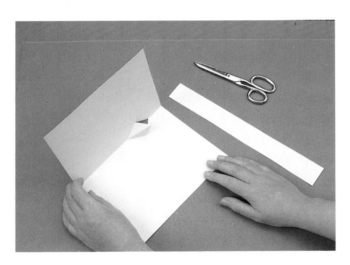

2 Make a single triangular opening in the fold of a 20.5cm x 28cm (8″ x 11″) piece of cardboard. (Follow the instructions for the frog on page 13.)

3 Draw and cut a triangle at one end of a strip of cardboard, to match the fold in the cardboard.

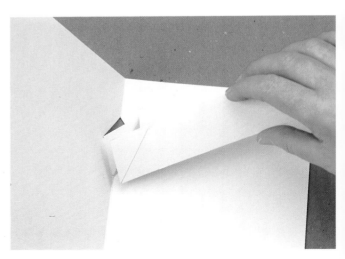

4 Glue the triangle then...

5 ...stick it firmly to the fold. Leave to dry.

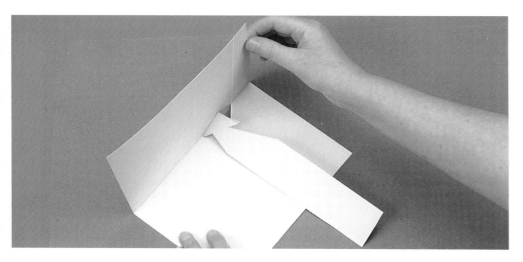

6 The strip will move down as you close the card.

7 Fold the card and...

8 ...cut off the strip that is showing when the card is closed.

9 Open up the card again and glue your picture to the strip of cardboard inside. If the cardboard strip is longer than your picture, cut off the extra cardboard.

10 As you open and close the card, your picture will move up...

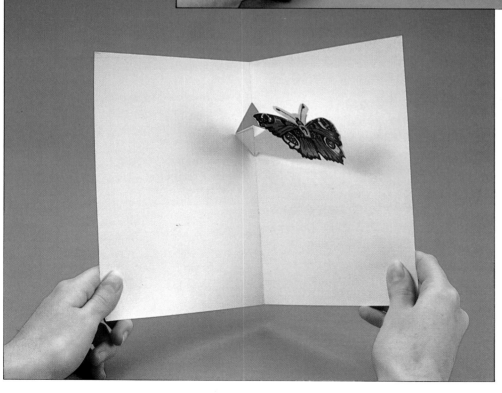

11 ...and down! You could finish off your card by adding some background scenery.

Pop-up pictures

Books with pop-up pictures have been popular since the middle of the 19th century. This idea shows you how to make your own pop-up design. You might like to make a special pop-up card for a special occasion – a surprise birthday card, or even a get well card.

You will need thin white cardboard, felt-tip pens, a pencil, a ruler, scissors, Elmer's glue, and a glue brush.

1 Fold a 20.5cm x 28cm (8″ x 11″) piece of the cardboard in half. Draw a picture (a building or a person) on another, smaller piece of cardboard.

2 Score and fold a strip of cardboard to form a box shape with a rectangular end. Glue this shape into the fold of your card as shown, so that the sides are parallel to the back and the base. Test to see if your card will fold flat, then leave to dry.

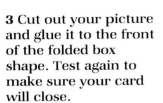
3 Cut out your picture and glue it to the front of the folded box shape. Test again to make sure your card will close.

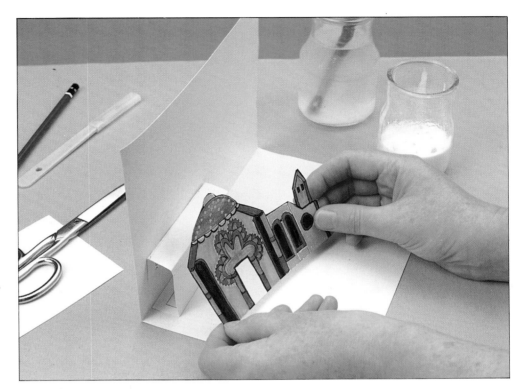

4 You can add to your picture by using another piece of cardboard folded in the same way. Here some trees are being added beside the castle.

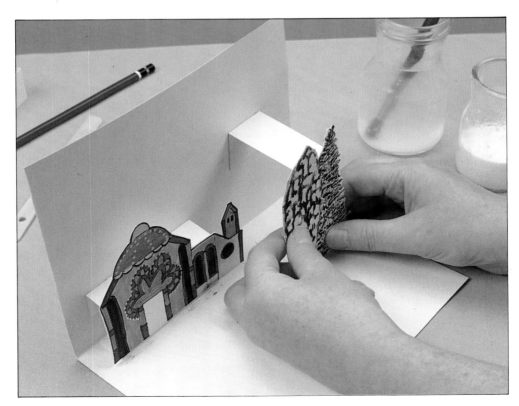

A pop-up toy

This is another pop-up idea to surprise your friends – a figure with a ping-pong ball for a head!

You will need a large plate, some thin fabric, felt-tip pens, scissors, a craft knife, a garden stake about 30cm (12″) long, a ping-pong ball, a needle, colored cardboard, Elmer's glue, a glue brush, a yogurt pot, colored wrapping paper, a rubber band, and yarn or ribbon.

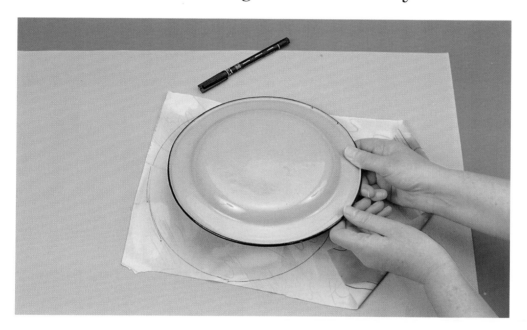

1 Use a large plate to help you draw a circle on the fabric. Cut out the circle. This will be the doll's dress.

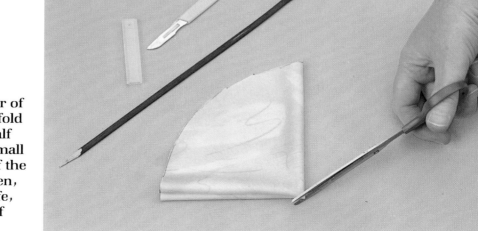

2 To find the center of your fabric circle, fold it in half then in half again. Cut a very small hole at the point of the fold, as shown. Then, using the craft knife, sharpen one end of the garden stake.

3 Draw eyes and a mouth on the ping-pong ball and make a small hole in the bottom with the needle.

4 Draw and cut out two hands with cuffs from a piece of cardboard. Here, a white cardboard template was used. Draw lines on the fabric circle to mark the position of the hands, as shown. Cut along these lines.

5 Glue the cuffs and push the hands through the cut lines from the inside. Hold to dry. Now push the sharpened stick through the center hole.

6 Push the pointed end of the stick through the hole in the ping-pong ball. Cover the yogurt carton with a piece of wrapping paper.

7 Make a small hole in the center of the base of the carton and push the stick through.

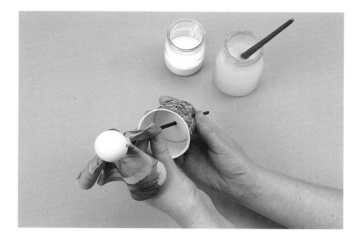

8 Using Elmer's glue, stick the bottom of the dress to the outside rim of the yogurt carton. Hold it in place with a rubber band while it dries.

9 Give your doll some hair. Use yarn, ribbon, or curled strips of paper. Attach the hair in position with glue.

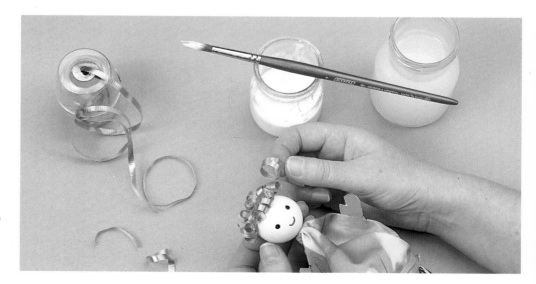

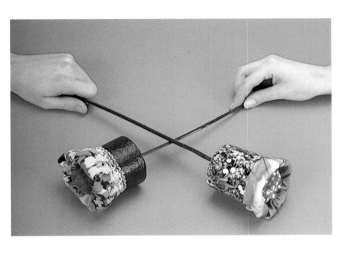

10 When your doll is dry you can pull it right back into the yogurt carton.

11 What a surprise when your doll pops up!

Making a still picture move

This picture is a rubbed crayon design which gives the impression of movement by repeating the rubbing several times. You will need thin cardboard, a pencil, scissors, Elmer's glue, a glue brush, heavy cardboard for mounting, paper, and crayons.

1 Cut a picture from thin cardboard, and glue it to a mounting board. Design your picture in two or three layers. This design shows an early steam engine.

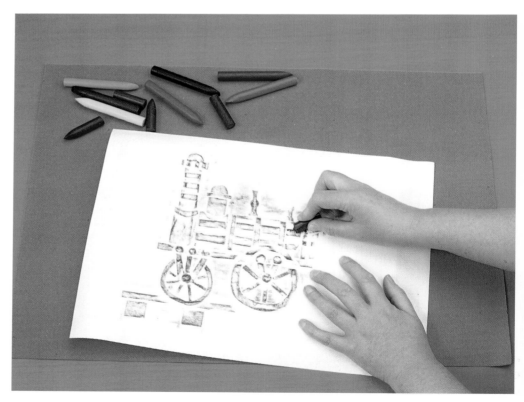

2 Place a sheet of paper over the board and rub across the raised design with the side of a crayon.

3 Move the paper along and make a second and third rubbing. Here the train appears to be slowing down.

4 Many rubbings create the impression of a fast-moving train.

5 Here is a clown design. You can see the raised surfaces.

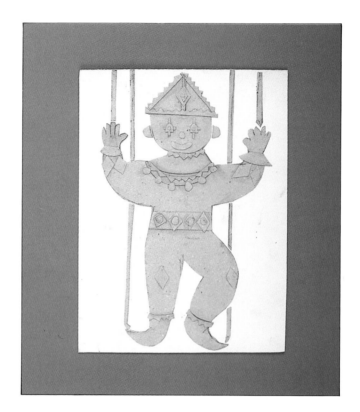

6 A somersaulting clown.

Moving images – a zoetrope

This toy dates from Victorian times. The word "zoetrope" comes from Greek words meaning "the wheel of life." When you spin the zoetrope, a series of still pictures appears to move, or come to life!

You will need thin cardboard, a paper plate, scissors, a pencil, a ruler, felt-tip pens, Elmer's glue, a glue brush, sticky tape, a long pin, a bead, and a bottle with a cork.

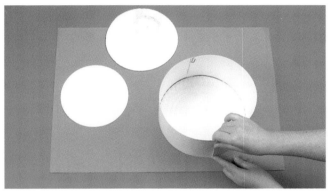

1 Cut a length of cardboard about 15cm (6") in height, and long enough to fit around the outside edge of a paper plate or cake board. (You may have to join two lengths of card together.)

2 Draw and cut slits evenly along the top of the length of cardboard, as shown. These slits should be about 5cm (2") deep and 1cm (⅜") wide. Draw a line 1.5cm (⅝") above the bottom edge of the cardboard.

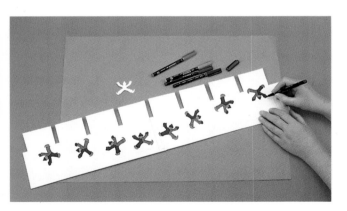

3 Draw a figure between and below each slit. Each figure should be in a slightly different positon. Here a clown is doing a somersault in eight progressive movements.

4 Make small triangular cuts along the bottom edge of the length of cardboard and up to the drawn line.

5 Fold up the tabs you have made then...

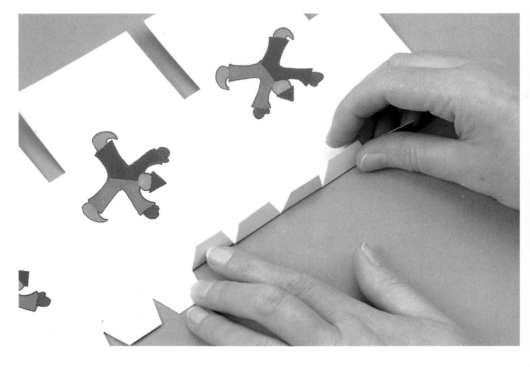

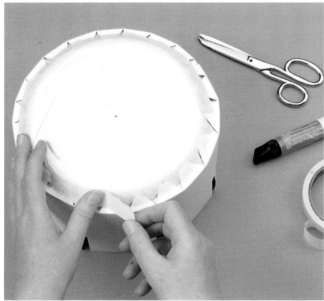

6 ...glue them around the outside rim of the paper plate. Attach firmly with tape.

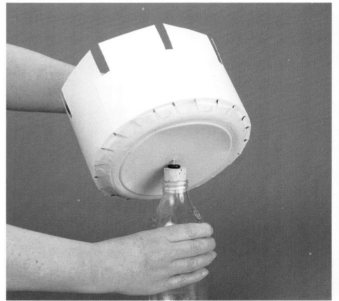

7 Push the long pin through the center of the plate. Thread the bead onto the pin before pushing it vertically into the cork in the bottle.

8 Holding the bottle firmly with one hand, spin the zoetrope and look through the slits. You will see your figure move.

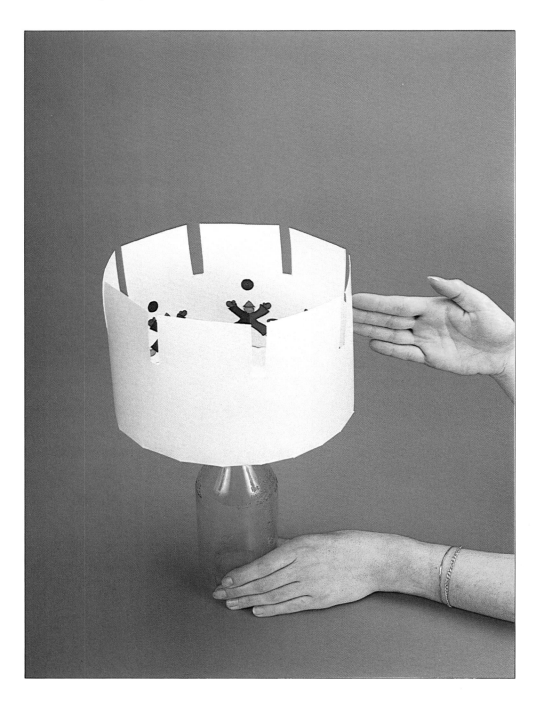

You can make other picture strips to fit inside your zoetrope. Here are some suggestions:

a) a juggler,
b) a runner,
c) a jumping horse.

This is another optical illusion. When you flip the pages of this book, the dot will appear to move.

You will need paper, cardboard, a pencil, a ruler, scissors, a felt-tip pen, and glue.

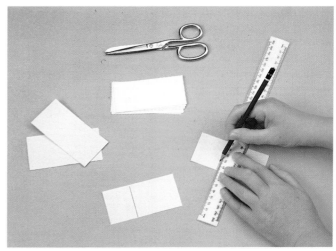

1 Cut thirty pieces of paper and two pieces of cardboard, each 5cm (2″) wide and 10cm (4″) long. The cardboard will be the book's cover, and the paper will be the pages. Draw a line 4cm (1½″) from one end of each page.

2 Using a felt-tip pen, draw a dot on the first page. Place the next page on top of the first so that you can see the dot through the page. Draw a dot on this second page so that it is in a slightly different position from the first.

3 Continue to make a dot on each page in the same way, so that each new dot moves slightly away from the one on the previous page. Place the pages in order, as shown.

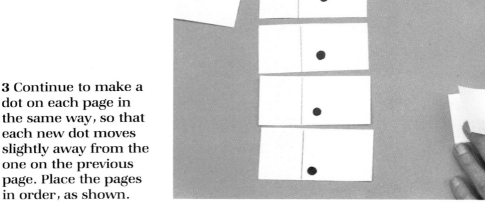

4 When you have made a dot on each of the thirty pages, work back from the last page to the first (remembering to keep the pages in order), and glue each page together on the other side of the line.

5 Glue a cardboard cover on both sides of your book. Leave to dry. Hold the book in one hand and flip through the pages with the other. The dot will appear to move.

Using the same technique, you could try to make a person move by drawing a slightly differently positioned figure on each page.

A circular spinner

This is another idea that shows how a picture can remain in the "mind's eye" even after it has disappeared. It is called a thaumatrope, from Greek words meaning "spinning wonder."

You will need cardboard, a compass, a pencil, scissors, white paper, felt-tip pens, glue, a needle, and thread.

1 Cut out two circles of cardboard, each with a 5cm (2″) radius. Draw two circles, also with a 5cm (2″) radius, on a piece of paper. Draw a person in one of the paper circles.

2 Cut out the circle with the person in it and place it *underneath* the other paper circle so that the picture shows through. Draw the frame of a house on the *top* circle, so that the person appears to be standing inside. Mark the top and bottom of both pictures with a dot.

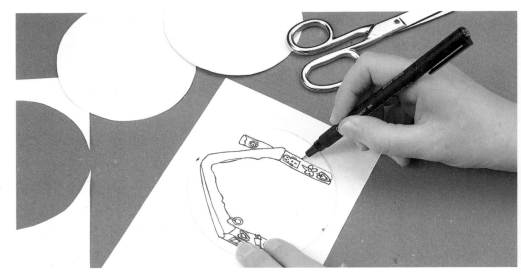

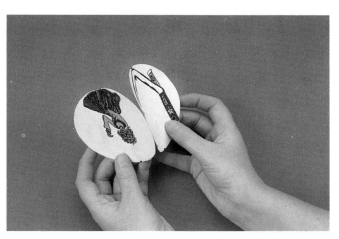

3 Cut out the second paper circle and color both pictures. Mount each picture on one of the cardboard circles, for support.

4 Matching the dots top and bottom, glue the pictures back to back so that one of the pictures is upsidedown.

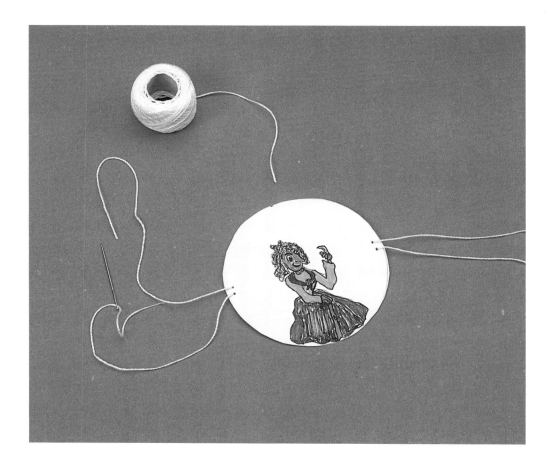

5 Using the needle, make two holes on either side of your spinner. Thread thin string through each side. Tie the ends.

6 Hold the spinner by the strings and swing it to twist the strings. As the strings rapidly unwind, the person will appear to be standing in the house! This happens because you see the second picture before your eye has forgotten the first.

Try to design some other thaumatrope pictures of your own. Here are some ideas
a) a bird in a tree,
b) a mouse in a hole,
c) a bee in a hive.

A twirling snake

To make a colorful spinning
snake you will need a small
plate, thin white cardboard, a
pen or pencil, felt-tip pens,
scissors, and a needle and thread.

1 Use the small plate
to help you draw a
circle on a piece of
cardboard. Draw a
spiral line inside the
circle to the center.

2 Draw the head of a
snake at the center,
then decorate the
snake's body with felt-
tip pens.

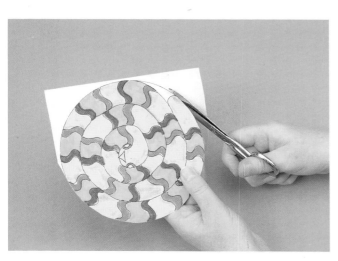

3 Cut out the snake
and...

4 ...cut carefully
around the spiral.

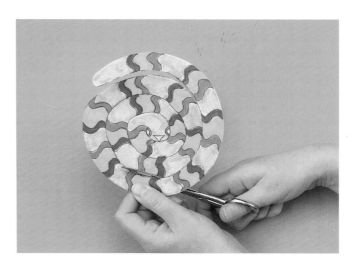

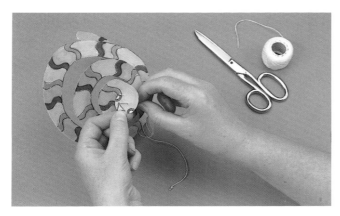

5 Using the needle, pull the thread through the center of the snake's head. Tie a knot at the end of the thread so that it does not pull through.

6 If you hang your snake over a warm radiator, the snake will spin. It moves in the current of rising warm air. (The snake on the left has been decorated with colored sequins.)

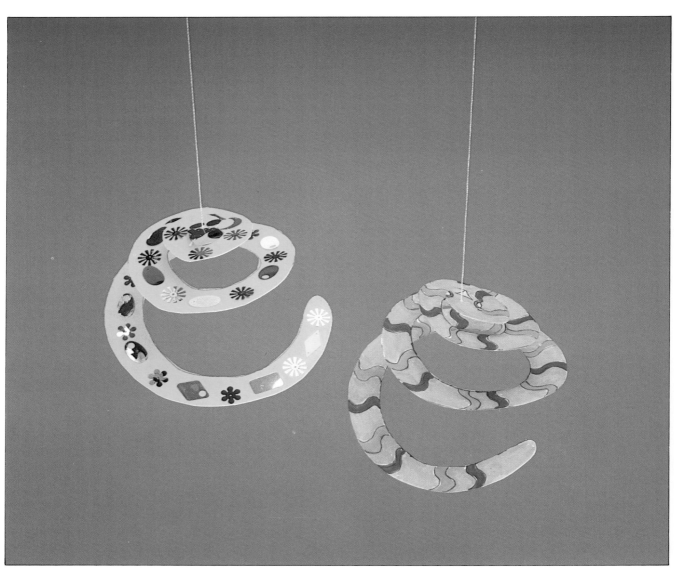

A twirling doll

This doll is called a "poupard" doll. Its name comes from French words meaning "doll without legs." Simple examples were made long ago, using a wooden ball on a stick. This was wrapped in cloth to represent a baby doll.

To make a poupard doll you need a plastic bowl, wallpaper paste and water, newspaper, a dowel rod, Elmer's glue, a glue brush, ribbons, thread, paints, a paintbrush, yarn, a needle and beads.

1 Mix a small quantity of wallpaper paste in the plastic bowl. Tear some newspaper into small pieces, and drop these into the paste. Stir well until the papier mâché mixture is stiff enough to mold into a ball shape for the doll's head.

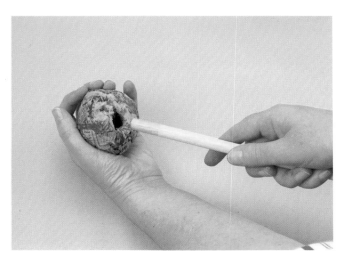

2 When you have made the head, hold it in one hand and push the dowel rod inside, almost to the top. Remove the rod, and leave the head to dry.

3 Glue about six colored ribbons to the rod at the place where the neck will be. Secure with thread.

4 When the head is dry, paint the head and the face.

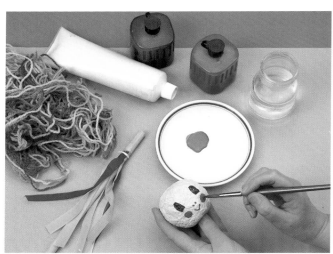

5 Glue the dowel rod into the head. Attach some yarn for hair, and sew beads to the ends of the ribbons.

6 As you twirl the doll, the beads will swing out on the ribbons.

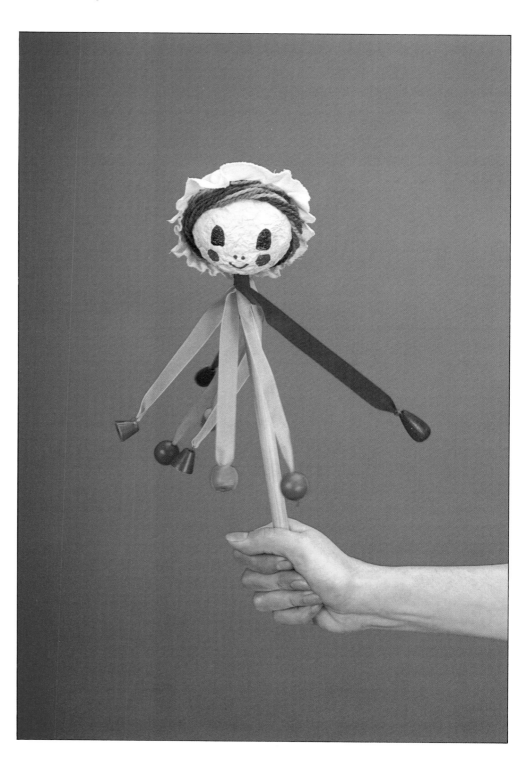

You could use bells instead of beads to make a musical doll.

1 An assortment of junk materials.

A walking fantasy creature

Here is a chance to be really imaginative and creative! You can use an assortment of junk materials such as paper plates, old boxes, cardboard tubes, and fabric scraps. You will also need paints, two matchboxes, some modeling clay, two strips of thick cardboard, a hole punch, thin string, and glue.

First, make a body from a cardboard box or tube. Use a paper plate, cardboard lid or paper cone for the head. (The head and body can be any shape you like. You choose!) Decorate your figure with paint.

Make two feet from matchboxes filled with modeling clay. This will make them heavy. Join the head to the body with a strip of material, and the feet to the body with string. Punch a hole at each end of the two cardboard strips. Glue them together to make a cross shape.

2 Join the head, body and "knees" of your fantasy creature to the cardboard cross. As you lift each leg and swing the heavy feet forward, your creature will walk!

Most of the materials mentioned in this book are easy to obtain.

Make your own collection of assorted waste materials (such as old boxes, waste packaging, scraps of fabric) and store them in a large box. Once you start looking, you will find all sorts of interestingly shaped cardboard packets and tubes!

Regular ping-pong balls are inexpensive.

Paper and cardboard
Most stationers stock a good range of paper and cardboard in different weights, textures and colors.

Special materials
Special materials such as oil pastels, beads, and sequins can be obtained from arts and crafts stores, or ordered through a schools' supplier such as J. L. Hammett, P.O. Box 545, Braintree MA 02184

Adhesives
Cold water paste (such as wallpaper paste) is suitable for sticking papers and lightweight materials. White glues, such as Elmer's, are suitable for heavier materials. For a more instant, quick-drying glue, try Duco Cement or UHU glue.
ON NO ACCOUNT SHOULD IMPACT ADHESIVES BE USED.

White glue can also be mixed with powder paint to produce an acrylic paint. This will give a shiny, more lasting finish to a painted model.

Scoring cardboard
In order to fold a piece of cardboard along a straight line, it is easier if you score the cardboard first. Place a metal ruler along the line to be scored, and make a firm cut with a craft knife. Do not cut through the cardboard. It will then be easy to fold your cardboard along the line.